ADS FOR AUTHORS WHO HATE MATH

WRITE FASTER, WRITE SMARTER

CHRIS FOX

CHRIS FOX WRITES, LLC

WRITE FASTER, WRITE SMARTER SERIES

5,000 Words Per Hour
Lifelong Writing Habit
Write to Market
Launch to Market
Six Figure Author
Relaunch Your Novel
Plot Gardening
Ads for Authors Who Hate Math

INTRODUCTION

Most authors hate math with the kind of revulsion reserved for telemarketers, but we want to sell more books, right? So we take expensive courses and read books, and try to wrap our heads around the whole process. Those of us with technical backgrounds fare better, but most authors lack that advantage. They don't want to be tied to multiple spreadsheets, and to calculating read-through rates and cost per click. The idea of split testing scares them.

But they know they need advertising.

So what's an author like that to do? How do you sell books if you hate math and can't juggle all the crazy numbers and metrics associated with platforms like Facebook or Amazon? In the second chapter we'll learn about the Aggregate Sales Model, which I capitalized because it's, like, super important and stuff. A cardinal rule, if you will. Don't worry. It isn't nearly as scary as it sounds. Basic addition and subtraction.

The short version? What matters most with your ads is if

you're making a profit, and you shouldn't need a degree in finance to determine whether or not you are. This book seeks to demystify the process and allow the average author to run a profitable advertising campaign.

Equally important, it will teach you to determine if advertising makes sense for you. **Many authors, put bluntly, cannot advertise profitably with their current backlist.** Their covers and their blurbs just aren't where they need to be. If you spend $10,000 advertising a book with a terrible cover and a boring blurb, then your conversion will be terrible and you'll be flushing that money down the hungry throats of Amazon and/or Facebook.

I've watched authors do exactly that, and then loudly proclaim that advertising is a waste of time. Don't be that author. Spend the time and money to ensure your cover is amazing. Workshop the heck out of your blurb. There are resources in this book to get you started on that, and I've got other books on those topics.

Only when your book is perfect should you consider advertising. Only then will the material in this book be useful to you. Assuming your covers rock, and your blurbs are tight, then we just have one more bit of business before we get started.

Before you buy a book on marketing, or advertising, or anything really, you should vet the author. Can they really do what they say they can teach you to do? Have they sold a shit-ton of books? Are they selling books right now?

The short answer in my case is yes, I have sold a shit-ton of books. And I am currently selling a shit-ton of books. You can find the longer more pompous version below.

About the Author

I published my first novel on October 25th, 2014. I didn't do it to make money, because at the time I was a fancy iPhone engineer working on super cool apps in the heart of the San Francisco tech world. I basically had no life, but made great money. So what was my motivation?

I wanted to impress a girl.

I'd just met the woman who I went on to marry, my wife Lisa. She'd read some of my fiction and was very encouraging, and I figured that chicks dig authors (wait, maybe that was athletes).

Anyway, because I worked in the tech world I understood how companies like Amazon were using data science to sell books. I theorized that if I published the right book, that I could leverage that data science to get companies like Amazon and Apple to sell my books.

Three hundred thousand readers later I feel pretty confident that I understand how the process works. The basics are covered in another book in this series, *Six-Figure Author*. The fundamentals of getting your book to where it will sell are covered in *Write to Market*. The book you're holding is the missing piece, though.

After reading SFA and WTM many authors came to me with the same question. I've got the book, and I know who my audience is, but how do I reach them?

The answer is advertising.

If you don't have a list, and you aren't friends with top authors in your genre, then your only real choice is to advertise your book. As brutally terrifying as that sounds—it's the truth. Advertising is a survival skill for authors.

I've spent the last five years mastering this process. I've used every platform from Google Adwords, to Facebook, to Goodreads, to BookBub, to Reddit, to Amazon, to—hold on, I'm starting to twitch. Flashbacks.

All that math stuff most authors hate? I steeped myself in it. I learned the data. I learned how to determine whether or not my ads were profitable. But I also realized that advertising that way is a full time job, and that all my fancy math wasn't telling me anything vital.

Authors don't have six hours a day to create and prune ads. Most can't even find one hour. So I started working on a solution. I theorized that I could come up with a system that would let me advertise profitably, but that wouldn't require me to sacrifice my precious writing hours.

You're holding the result. It's my hope that this book is a game changer for you.

-Chris

PART I

FUNDAMENTALS

IS ADVERTISING EVEN WORTH IT?

Before we go any further it's time to ask the hard questions.

Is spending money on ads a giant waste of time and energy for you? Should you even be advertising?

Because for almost every author the answer is that advertising is a waste of both time and money. I mentioned this briefly in the introduction but I feel strongly enough about it to make the topic into its own mini-chapter.

How Good Is My Backlist?

Every author, in the beginning at least, has a terrible blind spot. Our first novel is our baby. We pour our creative souls into the work, and like any parent we believe our child is special.

On some level we have suffered the quiet unease, the nagging feeling that maybe our cover isn't quite the best in the genre. But it's pretty good, right? Good enough, certainly.

You've got that part of the equation taken care of, right?

Be 100% certain. Ask author friends. Browse Amazon and look at the best-selling covers. Is yours ready for the big leagues? If the answer is no then do not collect $200. Do not pass Go.

You shouldn't be spending money on advertising, unless that money is to test how well your current cover performs. Unless it dramatically surprises you in a Rudy-style come-from-behind win, then turn the ads off and start saving up for the best cover in the industry.

There's absolutely no reason to settle. The best artists are expensive, and some have wait lists, but if you've got 90 days you can have the best artist in the world do your cover.

But what if you don't have $800, or $1,000, or whatever your genre's best would cost (some are much, much less expensive than that)? I completely empathize. I remember waiting for my tax return every year, because my checking account had $18 and I was eating a whole lot of ramen.

The best cover wasn't feasible, and that's fine. Save up until it is. Dumping a ton of money into ad spend will quickly drain your savings without accomplishing much else.

Make absolutely 100% certain that your cover is the best in the industry. I've got tips to do that in this book, and in the *Ads for Authors Who Hate Math* course you'll hear me squeeze into the conversation as naturally as I can.

You Are a Gambler

So let's say your cover is as good as it needs to be. Let's say you hired Tom Edwards or Chris Kallias to do your military SF novel. Let's say you've got killer original artwork for your epic fantasy, or the hunkiest of all hunks for your sports romance.

Now it's time to waste some money, and that's exactly how we're going to approach it. You're going to set a monthly ad-spend budget the same way you might give yourself a spending limit to gamble with in Las Vegas.

I'm not much of a gambler. I hate spending money in casinos. Adopting the cavalier attitude of 'easy come, easy go' isn't in my nature. It took me a lot to become okay with flushing money down the toilet on ad spend.

Wow, was it worth it. At first I said I'll spend no more than $5 a day. That $150 a month felt largely wasted, because I didn't move very many copies. But that wasn't the point.

The point was to teach me to be a better advertiser. The point was to learn to manage ads, and write better copy, and find better images. In short, I needed to build the advertising skill, and that costs money. Literally.

I became a gambler. $150 a month eventually became $3,000 a month, and there it stayed for about two years. In January I raised that to $7,000 a month, and it could creep up to $10,000 very quickly.

To reach the level where I could spend this kind of money profitably I needed to know my audience. I needed to know that my cover was the best. I needed to understand which ad platforms were worth my time.

A slow trickle of ad spend will teach you all those skills. If you commit to an affordable dollar amount each month, then before long you're going to answer some big questions.

First, you'll figure out whether your cover and blurb are good enough. Second, you'll learn whether or not you can do this profitably with your current backlist. Third, and perhaps most importantly, you'll learn how to create effective ads.

Some of your ads will fail. But some will mysteriously blow the doors off and get a super low cost per click. Each time one of these outliers occurs you will study it, and learn a bit more about why it did so well—which will help you make other ads that replicate its performance.

Take Charge of Your Learning

In this book you're going to see a lot of concepts. I'm going to say things like 'reduce the budget of that campaign by 50%'. I'm not going to include screenshots to do this on Amazon, Facebook, and BookBub, and the assumption is that you are already familiar with basic advertising platforms.

This book is about advertising principles, but learning specific platforms is up to you.

Every platform (except Reddit) contains a recommendation for further reading if that's the platform you choose. However, no amount of reading will teach mastery.

Practicing making ads does. Take the time to play with the platform(s) you think are worth using. Click all the buttons. Make ads, then delete them without running them. Try uploading images. If Facebook is asking you which type of ad to make, then make one of each. Play, play, play.

Along the way you're going to run into terms like CPC, ACoS, read-through, and a whole bunch of others. I've gathered as many of these terms as I can think of into the Lexicon at the end of the book. If you're not sure what I mean just flip back there, and you can find a definition for most terms.

If you find anything missing let me know and I'll add it!

$$\approx$$

Exercise #1- Commit to a Monthly Budget

Take a hard look at your cover and your blurb. Are they good enough? Show them to other successful authors in your genre, and see what they say.

If, and only if, they agree that your cover rocks, then decide on an affordable dollar amount. How much can you spend every month? $50? $500? Zero? The answer will be different for every author, and that's okay.

Come up with yours. Remember that this money will be lost every month. It's gone. Maybe you'll make some sales and maybe you won't. Treat this like an expense, and set it at a level you're comfortable with.

Bonus: Break your ad spend down by series. How much does each part of your backlist get? Why?

2

THE AGGREGATE SALES MODEL

I n a perfect world advertising would be simple. We would spend X number of dollars, and sell Y number of books. Either you make a profit, or you don't, and you can tell immediately if that's the case.

Unfortunately, the real world makes it nearly impossible to accurately track how effective any particular ad is. This is especially true if your book is enrolled in Kindle Unlimited, because there is no way to correlate when someone who borrowed your book read it.

If you run $100 in ads today, and 20 people borrow the book, but only 2 start reading right away, then what's your conclusion? You spent $100 for 2 sales. The ad isn't working. You can't see all the other people who borrowed, but who won't have time to dive into a good book until after work on Thursday.

If those other 18 book borrowers finish reading over the next three weeks you might break even or even make a profit on your $100 ad spend.

So how do we know which ad accounts for which page reads? Simply put, we can't. The closest we can get is forming a complex model where we track page reads from previous months and compare it to ad spend. I've talked with some of the finest minds in publishing, and we've beaten our heads against it for years. Not even Alex over at K-lytics has cracked it yet, and that dude is crazy smart, trust me.

And there's another problem complicating things...

Amazon Rewards Success

Let's say you spend $1,000 advertising your new release, and you sell $500 in books, and get $300 in page reads. *Counts on fingers* It looks like you lost $200. That sucks.

But wait a minute. You just sold a bunch of copies. Now your book has percolated Amazon's ecosystem. More importantly, while you were doing that Amazon was tracking the number of impressions it served. If it showed your book one million times, then it wants to know what percentage of those million people clicked on the book.

If the percentage exceeds a certain hidden threshold, then Amazon realizes they have something worth sharing. They'll cheerfully email people who like books like yours, people who signed up to be notified when you release a book, and really anyone else they think will buy it.

They'll craft dynamic landing pages so that when readers come back to pick their next read your novel is the one they see. Amazon does this because they like selling things, and they like happy customers. They want to give that customer what they want, and by selling that $800 in books we proved that we had something customers want.

All of a sudden Amazon sends flurries of emails. If lots of people click those emails, then they send more emails. And more emails. And show more landing pages. They will peddle the heck out of your book, which is where much of my profit as an author comes from.

We're theoretically $200 in the hole after our ad spend, but if Amazon spends the next three weeks sending emails on our behalf we might make another $800. Or $8,000. I've had both happen.

That's absolutely wonderful for your bank account, but how do you know which sales (if any) come from the ad, and which are from Amazon's efforts on your behalf? Maybe we would have gotten those sales from Amazon anyway, without advertising. Maddening, right? There's one more wrinkle, although this one isn't as bad as the others.

Audio & Paperback

If I'm advertising an ebook for *The Dark Lord Bert* there's a good chance that the person seeing the ad is an audio listener. If they are, then they're not going to buy the ebook. They're going to buy the audiobook.

Look inside ↓

The Dark Lord Bert Kindle Edition
by Chris Fox ~ (Author)
★ ★ ★ ★ ☆   78 customer reviews

› See all 3 formats and editions

Kindle	Audiobook	Paperback
$0.00 kindleunlimited	$7.47 or 1 credit	$8.99 ✓prime
Read with Kindle Unlimited to also enjoy access to over 1 million more titles	or 1 credit	7 New from $8.99
$3.99 to buy		

How does a 1-hit-point goblin become the Dark Lord?

By accident, Bert is a tiny goblin with big dreams. He follows adventurers, and loots the copper they leave behind when they take the real loot. One day, Bert hopes, he'll have enough copper to buy a warg, and finally promote from a 1-HP critter to a Warg Rider.
‹ Read more

▶ Audible Sample

However, they're still going to click on my ebook ad, and once there they'll click the audio option. The ad won't know that. All it knows is that they didn't buy the ebook.

Let's say I spend 30 cents a click, and I send 20 people to the page. I've spent $6. If only 1 person buys the book then it looks like I lost money. But what if another bought the paperback or the audiobook? A few will buy all three. None of those is linked to the ad, and if you look at Amazon's dashboard (for example) it will not reflect the audio sale in your ACoS (Average Cost of Sale).

You could be making a ton of money from both audio and paperback, but if you're tracking ads the conventional way, the math-heavy way, that won't be apparent at all. Facebook or BookBub will cheerfully tell you that your ad sucks and is draining your wallet, when in fact it could be generating a profit.

Enter the Aggregate Model

People who hate math are going to love this next part. All those spreadsheets and read-through calculations...just go right ahead and toss those. For now at least. Chapter 8 breaks down how they work, because it's valuable to know, but you won't need all that stuff day to day.

Let me give you the one formula you must commit to memory. It's super complicated, but I believe in you.

Revenue(Audio, Paperback, Ebook) - **Expenses**(Ad Spend, Production Costs) = **Profit**

That's the hardest math you're going to have to do, and it's the most important calculation you can make. Simply put, are you spending more than you are making?

Add up all ebook, audio, and paperback sales across all retailers to calculate total revenue, then go look at your dashboard wherever you are advertising to figure out how much you spent. Add in your cover and editing costs.

As long as your Revenue exceeds your Expenses you're in the black.

You don't need to know where the sales are coming from. You don't need to know if Amazon is sending out mailers on your behalf. All you need to do is make sure you're in the black.

I typically run monthly reports, and don't worry about day-to-day ad spend. Since I've committed to a specific number it's easier not to stress over it.

These reports take me less than 20 minutes, and when I say 'reports' I really just mean plugging in the numbers above and seeing how much I spent versus made.

Your turn.

Exercise #2- Calculate Your Gross Profit

Add up all revenue you earned from your books. This should include audio, print, and ebook.

Now add up all money you spent on marketing and advertising. Include every penny. Boosted Facebook posts, Book-Bub, AMS, whatever you spent rolls into that total.

Compare the numbers. Have you made a profit as an author?

Bonus: Break down each series and genre you write. How much did you spend to advertise each, and how much did you make? Which books or series are carrying your backlist?

3

30-MINUTE TIME BLOCKS

The title of this chapter is the mantra for the entire book. You shouldn't be spending more than 30 minutes a day working on your ads, unless you really enjoy advertising, or are setting up a massive campaign for a big launch.

For advertising to work it needs to be both understandable and a small enough burden that you can fit it into your existing routine. If you're spending an hour a day writing and 30 minutes advertising, then you've built the foundation for a successful career. Simply iterating every day will generate massive gains in your productivity, and eventually your profitability.

Put simply, you need a system. So what does that system look like? You're going to create a Time Block, and every day you're going to spend it in one of the following ways:

- Audience Building Day
- Ad Copy Day
- Image Gathering Day

- New Ad Day
- Pruning Day

Every day you're going to select the activity that makes the most sense. When your ads are performing you'll be experimenting with audiences. When your ads are doing poorly it's time for a pruning day. If you've got a new series coming out you're going to need both an image gathering day, and at least one ad copy day. Probably more.

Spending Time Blocks

So now that we get the principle let's look a little more closely at how you can spend your Time Blocks. If any of these activities are daunting, don't worry! We'll be breaking down every piece of this throughout the book.

Creating Audiences

Before I create my first campaign I need to know who I'm marketing to. Some platforms, like Amazon, have an automatic option for this that actually works pretty well. But not well enough that we can rely on it, or afford to ignore audience construction. **Understanding this one skill will make or break your career in the long term.**

If I'm working on an audience Time Block, then I'm sitting down and brainstorming a list of terms that describe the people who read my books.

My target reader is a 40-year-old male who is proficient at IT, and likely works in some sort of technical field. In short, my target audience is me. That isn't true in all cases. If you're writing in a genre outside your usual market, then it's very unlikely that your target audience shares your likes and predilections for fiction.

What movies does my 40-year-old male see? What books does he read today? What books did he read in 1985? 1995? 2005? 2015? What movies did he like during those time periods? What hobbies did he have?

Each of these will yield answers, and those answers are keywords. Those keywords will help us to construct our audiences. We will quite literally map out their interests over the course of their lives.

We'll cover that process later in the book, but for now it's important to see audience building as a siloed activity. When I'm building audiences everything else gets to wait until the next Time Block.

All I care about is audiences.

Gathering Images

Images, or the creative, as it is called in advertising, are probably the single most important part of your ad. If you pick the right images you will get a flurry of clicks regardless of what text you use, and those clicks are likely to cost you a lot less than if you used a bad image.

Because images are so important I recommend building a library of ones that work for your genre(s). This can actually be quite a lot of fun, and mostly involves browsing stock photo sites. If you've got the money, though, we also talk about building an art pipeline and what the advantages are.

Writing Ad Copy

Copywriting is vital to your success, and you have a lot more control over this skill than you usually do with images. We're already writers. Learning good copy is only a few steps from writing a good novel, and the skill can also be used to write your blurbs.

Practicing this skill is an excellent use of your Time Blocks, and we'll talk about specifics in a later chapter.

Making Ads

Once you have an audience and a library of copy and images it's time to make some ads. If you have none running, then you can create a single campaign and spend your 30 minutes filling it with ads. The beauty of this method is that your daily budget is the same no matter how many ads you are running.

Facebook can automatically feed budget to the best performing ads, and for other platforms you can manually do the same process. Which brings us to...

Pruning Ads

Pruning is the least fun part of the process, but just as important as any of the others. I usually schedule a pruning Time Block once or twice a week, and I spend the time reducing budgets on some ads, canceling other ads, and increasing budget on the ads that have performed well.

Understanding Crop Rotation

You want to structure your Time Blocks to support your backlist long term. Doing so requires you to understand the concept of rotation.

To continue the gardening metaphor I started in *Plot Gardening*, we need to rotate our ads like crops. If you have three series, then you're going to promote Series 1 heavily, then Series 2, then Series 3, then back to Series 1.

Here's how that breaks down practically. If you're a veteran advertiser you're familiar with campaigns. For everyone else they're simply a bucket to hold a bunch of ads. It's fairly typical to create a campaign for each book or series, and then group all your ads under that campaign. This is true for most platforms, though not all.

I start a campaign for each series whenever I'm about to run a promotion and / or have a new release coming out. I'll spend my Time Block creating ads in this campaign, and I'll do it every day for the launch window of my new book.

Eventually that series will begin to fall in rank and sales. This is what's known as the long tail. Advertising is how you lengthen that tail, and if you do it well you can usually milk about 60 days out of a typical release. After that Amazon is no longer helping to peddle your wares, or at least not nearly to the same degree.

By that point I either have another release in the same series, or I run a sale on one of my other ones. I'll create a campaign for the new series I want to promote, while still maintaining the first campaign at a reduced spend. In my case I have five series, which means that I can repeat this process often.

Every time a series begins to fall in rank and revenue, I either launch a new book or I put an older series on sale. This ensures that I'm regularly in the top 100 of my genre, which grants me a great deal of visibility.

Exercise #3- Schedule Your Time Blocks

Where can you carve out 30 minutes each day? If that's too daunting right now, then pick three days a week and schedule 30 minutes. That's 90 minutes a week you're investing in your future as an author.

Bonus: Add a tag to each Time Block telling you which activity you're going to work on. Are you building audiences? Pruning ads? Creating your first campaign? Lay it out in advance.

4

BUILDING AUDIENCES

We kind of have to start with audiences, because if we don't have an audience then who do we show anything to?

Your very first Time Block should be devoted to building an audience, or ideally several audiences. In this chapter we're going to talk about how to create them, then we're going to break down examples in different genres. I'm sure you can already guess what the homework assignment is.

Building an audience varies in complexity from platform to platform, but the principle is as simple as finding **people who like A and also like B.**

Location:	United States
Age:	25 - 65+
Gender:	Male
People Who Match:	Interests: Robert Jordan, Anne McCaffrey, Malazan Book of the Fallen, Terry Goodkind, Dragonlance, Dragonheart, The Wheel of Time, Mercedes Lackey, Jim Butcher, Dragonlance Legends, The Hobbit, A Song of Ice and Fire, Eragon, Record of Lodoss War, David Gemmell, R. A. Salvatore, Brandon Sanderson, High fantasy, Steven Erikson, Patrick Rothfuss, Sword and sorcery, Icewind Dale, Terry Brooks, Tracy Hickman, The Name of the Wind, Dragonriders of Pern, David Eddings, Shannara, Neil Gaiman, Joe Abercrombie, Tad Williams, Ursula K. Le Guin, The Lord of the Rings, Susan Cooper, A Storm of Swords, The Dresden Files, Scott Lynch, Raymond E. Feist, The Kingkiller Chronicle, Robin Hobb, Brent Weeks, A Dance with Dragons, The Eye of the World, Lev Grossman, The Way of Kings, Gardens of the Moon, Margaret Weis, Forgotten Realms, George R. R. Martin, Guy Gavriel Kay, Michael J. Sullivan (author), Glen Cook, The Stormlight Archive, The Farseer Trilogy, Cornelia Funke, The Sword of Shannara, A Feast for Crows, fantasy books, Peter V. Brett, The Sword of Truth, The Winds of Winter, New Beginnings (Dragonlance) or Mark Lawrence (author)
And Must Also Match:	Interests: Audiobook or Audible.com

In our case A is usually some combination of ebooks, kindles, or Kindle Unlimited. We build up a nice big chunk of people who like that, and then we narrow them down by saying also likes B, where B is whatever our genre is.

For example, let's say that I'm writing fast-paced thrillers. What search terms could I use that my target audience would recognize? I'd start with the Tom Cruise *Mission Impossible* movies. Hold on a sec while I go make this audience. BRB.

Looks like my final audience is 1.8 million people who like *Mission Impossible*, and also like ebooks.

Our whole job is to look for every possible intersection between something our readers will recognize, and our books.

Are you writing about superheroes? Wonderful. You can look up everything Marvel has ever made, and end up with several million people. You can create a slightly smaller audience for the D.C. films. You can even use the old school Image and Dark Horse brands.

The more nuanced your audience, generally, the lower your cost per click. If you zero in on a specific audience, and then show that audience exactly what they want to see, then your book(s) will sell like hot cake emojis.

How Do I Figure Out What My Audience Is Into?

Both of my examples are pretty cut and dried. It's easy to figure out which search terms to use, because we can reference big budget movies in well known genres.

But what if your book is niche? What if you have an archeo-logical-horror-thriller-sci-fi-adventure-romance like I do? My first novel is exactly that. *No Such Thing As Werewolves* was written after reading Donald Maas's *Writing the Breakout Novel*.

I was so sure I could blow the doors off the best seller charts by combining a bunch of genres, and the resulting book almost pulled it off. But how do you market that mess? Who do you market it do?

I went to the inspirations I'd used when writing the book. Back in the prehistoric dark of the previous millennium I used to play White Wolf's various pen and paper role-playing games. Imagine Dungeons & Dragons, but with more vampires, and a LOT more eyeshadow.

One of those games provided inspiration for my novel. I grabbed *Werewolf the Apocalypse* as a search term, and then added all the other games that company made.

Next I added Stephen King's *Silver Bullet*. My series has Lovecraftian elements, so in went H.P. Lovecraft, and the *Call of Cthulhu RPG*.

By the time I was done building this audience on Facebook I had a pool of 800,000 geeks who liked werewolves, eldritch horrors, and rolling dice in basements. I was tempted to add D&D players, or Rifts players, or any of a half dozen other roleplaying games that I'd played.

I resisted. The search terms I'd chosen all had a theme. They all fit into a very specific niche, a subset of interests that would intersect nicely with my book.

Separately, I built that D&D audience. These people are very similar to the first audience, but are after different emotional resonance. People play D&D more for adventure, and aren't as receptive to eldritch horror. They're fine that it's there, but using it to advertise to them won't be effective.

Instead, I included all the lighter roleplaying games I'd played over the years, and made this audience much more broad than the first one.

Finally, I built something completely different, a group of people who've probably never touched D&D.

This time I targeted people who loved Egyptology. I began with people who'd read *Temples, Tombs, & Hieroglyphs* which is the single most well known text on ancient Egypt, bar none. I added *Fingerprints of the Gods*, which posited that Atlantis was real, and that the pyramids might have been constructed via magic, or aliens. I added a dash of *X-Files*, and a hint of HP Lovecraft, and the show *Ancient Aliens*, and my third audience was complete.

Now, I had three distinct audiences, each with different hobbies and interests. However, all three have one thing in common. They all love to read, and they all do it on digital devices.

When I made these audiences I had no idea if they'd perform, but I had ideas on what each might like to see. I knew that the first audience had all seen *Lost Boys* and loved it, but that most of them rolled their eyes at *Twilight*'s sparkly vampires.

The second audience would mostly care that my werewolves had elaborate powers, castes, and abilities.

The third audience would care that I'd done my archeological homework, and had couched my mythology in real ancient world sites like Gobekli Tepe, the Great Pyramids, and Stonehenge. If my names, dates, and places weren't accurate they'd tear it apart.

Ultimately audience three is curious about mankind's origins, and love a convincing mythology about a long lost culture. The key word there is convincing, and I wouldn't dream of marketing to this audience if I didn't know the difference between Khafre and Khufu.

Age & Gender

Age and gender matter **a lot**. I've dropped ads from 35 cents a click to 9 cents a click simply by adjusting an audience to all men, or limiting the age in a narrow range from say 30-45.

But how do you know which gender(s) and ages to use? Test, test, test. You won't really know until you run a bunch of ads.

There's an easy way to do that.

We start by cloning all three of the audiences we've created, and then adjusting something simple on the new clone. For example, if we took the Egyptology audience and cloned it, we could set the clone's gender to men. We could clone it again, and make one for women.

Now the original targets everyone, and we have an ad aimed at men, and another at women. We can take our six audiences and further clone them, but this time we're adjusting the ages of the target audience.

You might set the age range from 18-34 on one set, then 35-65 on another. What you use should involve some common sense. If only really young people are reading your work, then having a 35-65 audience probably isn't worth testing.

Anyway, using this method we've created the following audiences:

Likes Werewolves
Men age 18 - 34
Men age 35 - 65
Women age 18 - 34
Women age 35 - 65
Both age 18 - 34
Both age 35 - 65

Likes Roleplaying Games
Men age 18 - 34
Men age 35 - 65
Women age 18 - 34
Women age 35 - 65
Both age 18 - 34

Both age 35 - 65

Likes Egyptology
Men age 18 - 34
Men age 35 - 65
Women age 18 - 34
Women age 35 - 65
Both age 18 - 34
Both age 35 - 65

Odds are really high that doing this took me at least one Time Block. I might not have even finished all three base audiences if I'm new at this. But however many sessions it takes, you want to focus on making a list like what you see above.

Now whenever we create an ad we can quickly and easily test it across 12 audiences. Over time we're going to spot trends. We'll learn which mix of genders, ages, and interests result in affordable clicks, and cheaper clicks mean more sales for less ad spend.

Exercise #4- Build Your First Audience

Review this chapter carefully, then create your first audience. Note that you don't have to plug this into any advertising platform, and can just jot it down on a napkin if you like.

The goal is to define an audience, then replicate it by age and gender. However, if you think you're going to use Facebook, or Amazon, or Bookbub, then try building the audience there.

You'll begin learning the system for the relevant platform. Age isn't used anywhere but Facebook or Google Adwords, but it's still worth having some idea as to the age of your ideal reader for those platforms.

Bonus: Define three audiences instead of just one. You're going to need them.

5

GATHERING IMAGES

Some phrases are so cliche that they've lost all meaning, despite being incredibly accurate. "A picture is worth a thousand words" is one of the worst offenders.

However, it's time for us to revisit that phrase. **A picture is worth a great deal more than a thousand words.** I'll go so far as to say that if your copy is perfect, but your image is not, then you've already failed. The reverse is not true. If your image is perfect, but your copy is not, then you will still sell books.

Without the right image you may not sell any at all, regardless of how good the actual book is. Let's look at why this is.

Symbolic Recognition

We don't often consider how we take in information as a species, or at least, most of us don't. I spend a lot of time thinking about communication, and about how we as humans process information.

Our eyes measure light. That's all they do. They parse radiation into colors, shapes, and textures. At first those colors mean nothing. When we're born we're incapable of understanding what all these fuzzy blobs mean, but eventually we start identifying shapes.

Very rapidly our brains notice patterns. We learn that if we see a nose, or eyes, or an ear, then we're looking at a person. Soon we realize that dude with the beard is dad, and the smiling lady is mom.

We learn what colors are. We learn that a red octagon is a stop sign (at least in the United States). The older we get the greater the library of symbols our brain has learned. Thousands upon thousands of symbols. Every word you know is a symbol. Every letter you know is a symbol. Every number you know is a symbol.

Orange. Bicycle. Elephant. Nine. Each word triggers a visual event in your mind. We can picture a bicycle. Or elephant. Or dragon. Or hot steamy hunk who wants to ravage me. Or spaceship. Or cowboy. Or lightsaber. Or animated cat.

Our job as advertisers is to leverage symbology. If we understand what symbols resonate with our audience, then it becomes as simple as finding lots of versions of that symbol.

For me that often means dragons or spaceships. I find dozens of each, and build a library for use in my ads. I do this because each image loses effectiveness over time. The first time someone sees it their brain will connect the symbol.

This recognition is a pleasurable experience for most people, and we've all felt it. *Hmm, that's interesting.* You do a double take. The second time you see it, if you didn't stop the first time, you might stop and check it out. But by the third? Or fourth?

Now the ad is annoying. People are tired of seeing it. Or apathetic. Neither will result in sales. But what if you have dozens of pictures that trigger the same kind of symbolic recognition? Every time a reader sees a given image for the first time there's a chance that it will be the one that gets them to stop and actually read your ad.

Some images will fare better than others. You'll be able to see which, because those will be the ads with the lowest cost per click. That tells you that particular image is valuable, and should be shown more often.

Stock Photo Sites

The first place I look for photos are stock photo sites. These sites often charge a nominal fee to use a specific image, and I can pretty quickly burn through a chunk of money buying images.

You can then use these images under the terms of the license, which will almost always mean they're safe to use in your ads. I'd recommend verifying that, of course.

My favorite site is Shutterstock. It has a ~$35 a month plan that will let you download 10 images, which will very quickly populate your ad library. If you winced at the cost you are definitely not going to like the Book Brush and Art Pipeline sections below, nor are you going to like the kind of money you're going to have to dump into ads every month.

One of the largest sites available is called iStock. It's far, far more expensive for almost every type of image, but it's maintained by The Getty who have the largest collection of art in the world.

If you can't find what you need on Shutterstock, you might take the financial hit and grab something on iStock.

Book Brush

This section will be viewed as a straight-up commercial by many authors, and I applaud you on your skepticism. Always assume someone is trying to sell you something, and know that there are less expensive alternatives to Book Brush like Canva. That said, I like Book Brush because of its ease of use.

Book Brush is far easier and faster than finding your own images. Unfortunately, that comes at a cost. Book Brush currently costs $99 for a year. It's worth it for authors in many genres, particularly if you're going to need to make a lot of ads quickly.

You can learn more about their service at bookbrush.com, but here's a screenshot of the interface. You make a simple graphic, and can of course upload your cover or browse their immense image library, then add text or effects.

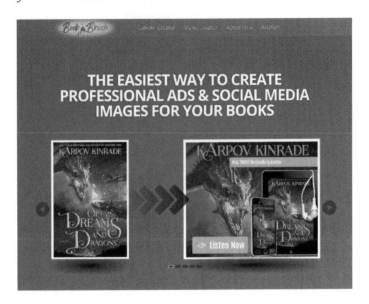

It's simple and fairly straightforward. Definitely a time saver, but fair warning: If you sign up to their service using the link above I get a kickback.

I only recommend services I believe in, but I'm finally coming around to the idea that it's okay for me to make money telling authors about useful stuff.

Check it out, but do not feel obligated to purchase the service, or any other service, unless you are flush with capital. Guard your author dollars like Scrooge McDuck. Be a miser.

But the second you've got the capital look for tools that will optimize your workflow. Tools like Book Brush.

Setting Up an Art Pipeline

The final option for artwork is the most expensive, by far. It's the route I've personally chosen, and I am investing $20-30k a year in artwork. I'm also trying to raise that figure.

My goal is to own several hundred pieces of amazing fantasy and science fiction artwork that reflect my unique universes and brand.

One of the uses I put the artwork to is my book covers, but the more frequent application is for my advertising. If I spend $300 getting a custom scene from the Magitech Chronicles, then any fans of the series will like, share, comment, and buy from that ad. They love new content.

Setting up an art pipeline is pretty straightforward. I head over to deviantart.com or artstation.com and start searching for the keywords we harvested back in the audiences chapter.

If your readers like cowboys, then search for every adjacent term at these sites. Horses. Guns. Trains. Etc.

Model Shoots

The last approach to generating massive images is a model shoot. The person who has crushed this is Michael Cooper. He booked a female model to play his protagonist, then took hundreds of photos of her in various poses holding rifles, etc.

If you hire a model, then you can generate an entire series worth of images in an afternoon. It can keep you advertising for months.

There are modeling agencies in every major city, and tons of models would love to be your protagonist.

Exercise #5- Gather Some Images

Make a list of words that represent your genre. These can be freeform, and more is better. Put on some music and go nuts. Here's 60 seconds from one of my series:

Dragons
Spaceships
Marines
Gods
Magic
Stars
Astronomy
Spells
Fighters
EVA
Aliens

Your list can be much longer, but make sure you have at least ten. What are the cornerstones of your genre? Rank your keywords in what you're guessing will be the order of popularity.

Find at least three pieces of artwork for the top three on your list, even if you can't afford to purchase them at this time.

. . .

Bonus: Replicate this for the entire list. The more artwork you have to test, the better.

6

WRITING GOOD AD COPY

Entire books have been written on copywriting. There are tons of rules, both spoken and unspoken. There are rival schools of thought, and arguments over whether or not scarcity in ad copy is valuable or detrimental. Arguments over everything, really.

After reading a massive body of work, though, I finally realized that the process was a good deal simpler than I was making it. At the end of the day all you need to remember is your reader.

Stop being author you. Take off that hat, and pretend like the most exciting thing in the world is discovering a new fictional world to escape into. Your day job sucks. Your boss doesn't appreciate you. If you have a spouse, they are overworked, tired, and grumpy. Life—real life—is a dreary place. The people who read the most usually read to escape. That's certainly true of most genre fiction.

Or they read to improve, which is true of most non-fiction. They want to better themselves, or learn about people who've done fascinating things. Each genre has its own needs, and knowing them before you write your blurb is key.

What does your reader want? What symbols will resonate with them? Tease them with a tagline. If that tagline works, then and only then will they read the blurb.

Hook Them in Six Words or Less

Six words can make your career. By the end of six words you need to plant an idea in your reader's subconscious by touching one or more of the symbols they're interested in. Say you're writing a book to teach people to advertise, like I am.

What do my readers want? What would cause them to pick up this book, and how could I do it in six words or less? Here were some of the taglines I brainstormed:

- Run ads in 30 minutes a day
- Stop wasting money on ads
- A simple system for ad management

Each of these is fine. Not amazing, but not terrible. Each touches on the reason you picked this book. You want to run ads, but the material you've read or watched so far hasn't given you the confidence to do that.

You've learned some concepts, and understand how the process is supposed to work, but you haven't quite taken the plunge. It hasn't quite clicked.

Obviously that isn't true for everyone reading, but I suspect it is for a lot of you. I've been an author for decades. I know what it's like to hunt endlessly for that one perfect book on a topic. My *Ads for Authors Who Hate Math* tagline is being written for author me from five years ago.

I looked at my taglines, and realized what was missing. I needed to convey that my book was different. My book will teach you in a way that the others will not.

Help! My Facebook Ads Suck by Michael Cooper is an awesome book, but only if you're using Facebook. Mark Dawson's course is amazing, but it's expensive, and it is a LOT of math and tracking.

I realized that if I were going to sell copies of this book I needed to convey that my book would solve the problem other books would not, and do it in a granular, easy to implement way.

So how do I do that? I started with the book's tagline. Ads for Authors **Who Hate Math**. That tells you right off the bat that this book is going to be simple, and that you are going to be able to understand the process described.

I brainstormed another set of taglines for the blurb:

- Stop losing money on your ads
- Learn to advertise effectively...without spreadsheets
- Advertising for the rest of us

I'm playing off the twin human drives, what zen refers to as longing and loathing. **We are always trying to either push something away, or bring something closer.**

Stop losing money on your ads capitalizes on that loathing. You don't want to waste money on ads. No one does. This tagline tells the reader that if they read the book **they'll avoid pain**.

Learn to advertise effectively without spreadsheets. Suggests that you will learn to manage ads in a profitable way, but that it won't be so complicated that you can't understand it. This tagline tells the reader that if they they read the book **they'll get pleasure**.

When writing non-fiction the first tactic is generally more effective, in my experience. People will do a lot more to avoid pain than they will to get pleasure.

If I hand you a coin and say that if you get heads I'll give you $1,000, then you're going to eagerly flip that coin. You've got a 50% chance of winning a nice wad of cash.

If I hand you a coin, and then hand you $1,000, and say that you only get to keep the money if the coin comes up heads... now you're stressed. You're about to potentially lose a whole bunch of money.

It's the same game. You have the exact same chance of walking away with $1,000. One of them is fun, and one is stressful. One of them is **longing**, and one is **loathing**.

Let's take a look at a longing example, since we're going to be using this much more often for fiction. We need to convince the reader that they're going to love this experience, and we need to do it in six words or less.

Here are some of my recent taglines. Note that sometimes it is okay to go beyond six words. There are no copy police who will swoop down if you use seven words. Just be aware that the longer you make it, the greater the chance the reader has already moved on.

"WARNING: May contain werewolves." —No Such Thing As Werewolves

"After 26,000 years the Void Wraith have returned. The next Eradication has begun." —Void Wraith Saga

"How does a 1HP Goblin become the Dark Lord? Hilariously." —The Dark Lord Bert

"Over 1,200 pages of Dragons, Starships, and Dead Gods." —The Magitech Chronicles Quadrilogy

"The Godswar has come again." —Krox Rises

Notice that several of these are longer than six words, but also notice what you've learned in the first six words. I'm going to bold symbols.

- **WARNING**: May contain **werewolves**
- After **26,000 years** the **Void Wraith**
- How does a **1HP Goblin** become
- Over **1,200 pages** of **Dragons**, **Starships**
- The **Godswar** has come again.

In every case we've used symbolic recognition from the last chapter. More importantly, we're stacking it. Remember that our reader isn't reading this tagline in isolation.

For the first one, WARNING: May contain werewolves, we've just seen this cover:

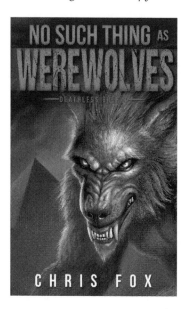

My reader sees the following symbols. WEREWOLF. PYRA-MID. They read the tagline. We've all seen 'Warning: May contain...' labels. And we're clearly juxtaposing that with the title *No Such Thing As Werewolves*.

The title says there are no werewolves, but there's a werewolf on the cover and in the warning. That's funny. That piques people's interest. They're curious.

What's this about? And why is there werewolf hanging out near a pyramid?

My tagline has promised the reader answers to these questions. Answers that, theoretically at least, they're going to learn in the blurb.

This book isn't about writing blurbs, unfortunately, so I'm not going to break that process down. Almost 100% of the copy you'll be using for your ads will come from taglines, so that's the part I think is worth most of your time and attention.

Learn to write great taglines and your books will almost sell themselves.

Exercise #6- Write Some Taglines

What kind of tagline will your audience respond to? Can you use longing or loathing? Which will work better? Write 10 taglines using either longing or loathing, whichever you think will work better.

Bonus: Write 10 taglines for either longing or loathing, whichever you didn't already do. The goal is to practice both. By making a bunch of each you'll force yourself to consider your plot or content from many different angles, which has a high likelihood of jarring loose a great phrase you can use.

7

TYPES OF ADS

W e now have all the component pieces! We've got an audience. We have images. We have some copy. We can make ads!

Building good ads isn't nearly as difficult as most people assume. At least, it isn't hard if you have a good system in place for creating said ads. This chapter provides that system.

Let's jump in!

Campaign Goals

Before you design your first ad you need to ask yourself what you're trying to accomplish. Most of my ads are aimed at direct sales. They go straight to my Amazon or Audible sales page, and are designed to get people interested enough to click that buy button.

Some of my ads are designed to deepen my audience and

brand awareness. In short, I want more people in my target audience to know who Chris Fox is and what I write about.

This quickest way of accomplishing this is through content marketing. Content can be a reader magnet novella you wrote. It can be character sheets. It can be a book trailer. You're giving readers something they're genuinely interested in, and are trying to get their email address in exchange.

Once you have their email, you start an autoresponder sequence to tell them all about you and your books, after giving them whatever they signed up for, of course.

If you're not a *Newsletter Ninja* I recommend picking up Tammi's book with the same name. That will tell you everything you need to know about setting up sequences and managing your email in general.

Ad Types

Once you've decided the purpose for your ad campaign it's time to make some ad variants. Presumably you've done the exercise in the last chapter, and now have at least one audience to work with.

Let's use my Egyptology audience. In order to reach them I want to try a variety of emotional appeals. People read speculative fiction to scratch various itches, but all those itches are emotional in nature.

Our ads need to signal that emotional appeal. There are four general vehicles for doing this, and I recommend testing all four.

- Sales Copy

- Quote
- Excerpt
- Comparison

Sales Copy

Sales copy is the marketing-speak we've all learned to distrust, and it's something that doesn't usually perform as well for me. Sometimes, though, it can work exceptionally well.

If I'm running a time-sensitive promotion I lean hard on this tactic with something like:

> "In 59 days our world will end. Join the fight for survival. Over 200,000 copies sold. 1,700 five star reviews. Buy now, before the book returns to full price!"

I've got a simple tagline, then I add some social proof, and then I use some scarcity to let them know that they'll be missing an opportunity if they don't buy now. Personally? I dislike this tactic. It can feel exploitive and doesn't fit my brand.

Your mileage may vary, and I've seen plenty of people use this kind of copy to great effect.

Reddit hates these ads with a passion. Facebook and Amazon are more tolerant, while BookBub seems to respond positively.

Quotes from Reviews

This one is a lot more fun. I browse my reviews searching for interesting reader comments. Whenever I find one I pull it out and use it. My favorite recent example was from *The Dark Lord Bert*. A reader called it "The Deadpool of GameLit."

That ad copy has killed for me. So have many other reader quotes. I also tend to make up quotes, and then tag them with 'the author's totally biased friend' (if you're going to steal that, I recommend tweaking it slightly. Readers can be vengeful if they think an author is plagiarizing).

These quotes should be short and pack a lot of punch, and it's okay to use two or more in the same ad, as long as the first one is catchy on its own. These ads convert very well for me on Facebook, and on Amazon. They don't do nearly as well on BookBub, and I'm still testing on Reddit.

If you choose to run quote-based ads, one of your Time Blocks can be devoted to mining your reviews and making a text document full of reader quotes.

Excerpt

You know that one scene that you wrote that just killed it? The one that you are super proud of, and that gets high-lighted and commented on? That scene can sell a lot of books.

Excerpt ads include 2-3 intense pages from one of your best chapters. This should be chosen so that the reader isn't too lost, but if selected, well wow, do these puppies convert. People get a chance to see what your prose is like, and if they approve they're all too happy to jump in and keep reading.

These ads convert best on Facebook, as Amazon and BookBub don't give you enough real estate to include a large enough amount of text. Reddit does, but my initial tests have not been promising.

Comparison

Comparison ads were hugely popular back in 2015, because Mark Dawson released his now famous ads course, and the free video leading into it recommended this tactic.

It's very simple. Pick the 800-pound gorilla in your genre, and compare your work to theirs. It's like Stephen King, but better! It's like J.K. Rowling and Stephanie Meyer had a beautiful love child!

You're taking something the reader is familiar with, and then relating it to your book. If your fans like *Harry Potter* or *Lonesome Dove* or *The Sisterhood of the Traveling Pants* then you use that in your ad copy, but compare that to your book.

This tactic is safest to use on Amazon, BookBub, or Reddit since people can't comment on your ads. If you use it on Facebook you're going to get unkind comments from fans of whoever you are referencing, but you're often going to sell books.

～

Exercise #7- Create Your First Campaign

Decide whether you are aiming at sales or sign-ups. You can actually create the campaign on a live platform if you've already got a one picked out. Note that you don't have to turn this campaign on, or give it any budget yet.

If you don't have a platform picked out that's okay. Create a document in whatever format you'd like to use (I love Google Sheets). Pick one type of ad from the list below:

- Sales Copy
- Quote
- Excerpt
- Comparison

Write three variants of that ad. That can mean finding three quotes, three excerpts, three comparisons, or three different sales copies, but make sure all three are of the same type.

Bonus: I highly recommend doing this step. Create three ads for each of the other types, even if you don't think you will ever use that type. Learning how to generate that copy is building a vital skill. Practice this often, and always be increasing the size of your marketing document.

8

OH NO, MATH

Before we get into some actual advertising I want to offer a bit of math that I think is worth your time. Tracking read-through is an important skill long term, because you really ought to know how your various books and series are performing in relation to each other.

Some people are too overloaded to do this, and that's okay. You can skip this chapter if you'd like. Likewise, those who've been tracking read-through for a while can jump to the next chapter.

You won't actually be using any of this in the aggregate sales model, but since it is important to running a business it's best you understand how it works.

Calculating Read-Through

Read-through simply refers to the percentage of people who read past the first book. You can compare the number of sales for book 1 against all the other books, and get a ratio.

For example, my Magitech Chronicles looks something like this:

Tech Mage: 100 sales

Void Wyrm: 74 sales (74%)

Spellship: 72 sales (72%)

War Mage: 69 sales (69%)

Krox Rises: 111 sales (111%)

I'm getting the percentage numbers like this:

Void Wyrm Sales / Tech Mage Sales

Or

74 / 100 = 74%

You repeat this math for each book. Divide the sequel sales by the first book sales to get your percentage.

Krox Rises is my latest release and is outselling the first book, so I can't calculate read-through accurately yet, but I suspect it will be somewhere around 67%, so that's what I'll use. Here's how you use those numbers.

Tech Mage: $0.33

Void Wyrm: $2.79 (74%)

Spellship: $3.50 (72%)

War Mage: $3.50 (69%)

Krox Rises: $3.50 (67%)

For every person who buys book 1, 74% will go on to buy book 2. I multiply my read-through times what Amazon pays me, and that gives me my estimated profit on the series.

That breaks down like this:

Tech Mage: $0.33

Void Wyrm: $2.79 * .74 (the read-through) = $2.06

Spellship: $3.50 * .72 = $2.52

War Mage: $3.50 * .69 = $2.41

Krox Rises: $3.50 * .67 = $2.34

For every sale I earn a theoretical $9.66, because about two thirds of the people who pick up the first book are going to read all the way through. That number goes up a couple bucks every time I release a sequel, which makes advertising more and more profitable.

If your books are enrolled in Kindle Unlimited we're not done, because we also have page reads to track. Normally my read-through percentages would be different (they're much higher than sales read-through), but for the sake of simplicity I'm using the same ones we did above.

Tech Mage: 354 pages

Void Wyrm: 310 pages * .74 = 229

Spellship: 344 pages * .72 = 247

War Mage: 346 pages * .69 = 238

Krox Rises: 360 pages * .67 = 241

This means that, on average, I'd have 1,309 page reads for every person who finished the series. Last month's KU payout was .44, so that means every borrow of *Tech Mage* nets me $5.76.

For those curious the actual payout is $7.18, and should go up to about $9.32 when Nefarius releases. The actual number isn't as important as understanding how to calculate it for your backlist.

Calculating Your Kindle Unlimited to Sales Ratio

We know how much we make from a KU read, and we know how much we'll get for a sale. But how do we use those numbers? We still need to determine how many people read in Kindle Unlimited, versus buy the books outright.

For most authors I know, the ratio is something like 2/3 of their ebook income is Kindle Unlimited and only 1/3 comes from sales. Calculating this is fairly simple.

(Pages / (Sales + Pages)) * 100 = KU percentage

If you plug in your sales revenue and your page reads, and then do this step by step on a calculator:

So, let's say we made $500 from sales, and $300 from KU.

500 + 300 = 800

300 / 800 = 3.75

3.75 * 100 = 37.5%

Your Kindle Unlimited page reads are 37.5% of your revenue, making your sales 62.5%. Make sense?

If you know that 2/3 of your money comes from sales, then that's the market you want to cater to. If, on the other hand, 2/3 of your money comes from Kindle Unlimited then your ads should be created with that in mind.

Exercise #8- Calculate Read-Through

If you only have one book out, or aren't enrolled in Kindle Unlimited, congrats! You get a pass.

If you have more than one book, and those books are in a series, then use the formula above to determine how much money you'll make for a sale, and how much you'll make for a read-through.

Also figure out what percentage of your revenue comes from sales versus page reads.

There is no bonus.

PART II

PLATFORMS

9

FACEBOOK ADS

I've decided to list the platforms in order of importance. Some authors will tell you that Facebook is their best ad platform. Some will say Amazon. It's tough puzzling out which is better, as both are large and mature.

Most people agree, though, that Facebook is the most powerful. Facebook is the epitome of Big Brother, and Big Brother is always watching. Every web site, every search term, and yes, even if you have incognito mode on.

Facebook has an utterly massive data profile on almost 2 billion people, and if you use Facebook you're one of them. As terrifying as this is, it is also incredibly useful to you as an author.

If you understand exactly who your target audience is, then Facebook can find them for you, almost instantly. I've watched countless authors brute force their way into the top 100 on Amazon simply through a large FB ad spend.

My favorite tool is retargeting. You know how you'll be browsing on a site that is in no way related to Facebook—

say, a bridal site—and then you log onto Facebook and all the ads you see have to do with weddings?

That's retargeting, which we will talk about in Part 3. It is incredibly useful, especially if you have long series.

Facebook Pros

- Fast reporting
- Granular audiences
- Nearly every reader you interact with has an account
- Allows the ability to retarget using a pixel

Facebook Cons

- Can burn through your budget quickly
- Only as effective as the audiences you create
- Highly competitive
- Desensitized audience

Where Do I Find It?

From your Facebook account click the drop-down on the upper right side, and scroll down to either 'Create Ad' or 'Manage Ads'. Note that this location could change, so you might have to explore a little.

How Do I Make An Ad?

Fair warning for this chapter and those that follow. I was initially against adding walk-throughs, because ad interfaces change often and anything I show you could be different by the time you're making an ad. Hopefully that's not the case!

When you first log in to Facebook ads you'll see part of the screen that looks like this. Tap that green 'Create' button.

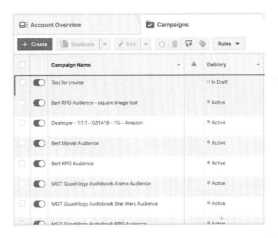

I recommend this button because it is the quick creator, and is much less confusing than other ad creation methods. Name your campaign, and if you are going to be doing a bunch of ads in this campaign I recommend turning on 'Campaign Budget Optimization'.

From there you can enter an Ad Set name like *Women 18-34 who like roleplaying games*. After you hit 'Save to Draft', Facebook will allow you to create the first ad, and you can create as many more as you'd like.

If making ads is daunting, then I recommend you consider the Ads for Authors Who Hate Math Course (https://chris-fox-writes.teachable.com/p/ads-for-authors-who-hate-math/?product_id=1083069), which has video walk-throughs of every part of this process.

When Should I Use Facebook?

Facebook has an incredibly powerful audience creation engine, and one of the largest pools of users on the globe. It is an amazing ad platform, and if not for one critical difference it would be the undisputed king.

Amazon users are on Amazon to buy. If they are readers,

then they are usually there specifically to buy books. This means that your audience is already warmed.

On Facebook you have to warm them yourself. This can be done with a low spend ad run for a long period of time, but it can be done faster by giving readers something fun.

Check this trailer for *The Magitech Chronicles*. It's less than 30 seconds, but it quickly and intuitively gets the magic system across. It's not a video link, but if you want to see you it you can check it out at magitechchronicles.com/magic-the-circle-of-eight/.

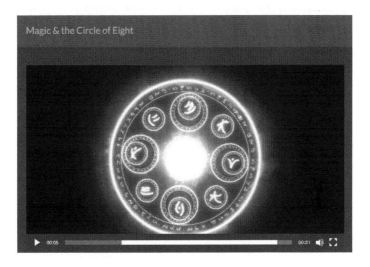

Note that there's no catch to this. It's just a trailer. A Facebook user has no barrier of entry. They thought it looked cool, clicked on it, and watched it.

Some of my trailers have an ad for the books so they know they exist, but few users buy right then. Instead, a couple days later, I use everyone who clicked on the video as a new audience.

I know these people thought the video was cool enough to warrant a like or share, and I know they like science fiction & fantasy. More importantly I know that not only do they read, but they do it on digital devices. This pool of users has the greatest likelihood of buying my books.

Retargeting is explained in Part 3, but I wanted you to understand the basics as this might be the most powerful tool Facebook offers.

Further Reading

I highly recommend *Help! My Facebook Ads Suck* by Michael Cooper. Michael walks you through the basics of creating Facebook ads, and you can read the entire book in an hour or two.

His book put me on the path to profitable Facebook ads, and much of my experimentation is built on his methodology.

Exercise #9- Set Up a Facebook Ads Account

It doesn't matter if you ever plan to use it, or if you don't have a budget to spend on Facebook. Basic familiarity with this ad platform could be important to your career as an author. Lots of people use it, and it isn't likely to change soon.

Note that this requires you to have a Facebook account.

. . .

Bonus: Make and save three audiences in Facebook using what you learned in the building audiences chapter. If it's unclear how to do this go to Google and search for "Make Facebook Audience 20XX" where XX is the year.

Yes, I could include the information here, but you need to be able to research topics, and this is great practice.

10

AMAZON ADS

Amazon is my favorite ad platform simply because it is the fastest and easiest for creating new ads. When I launch a new book I can get Amazon to eagerly drain my bank account with just a few clicks.

Unlike other platforms Amazon has amazing auto-targeting options. Their data science division might not know anything about facial recognition, like Facebook, but no one knows how to sell things like Amazon.

Unfortunately, every author on the planet seems to already know this. Back in the day (2015) Amazon ads were a literal joke. No one was using them. Then Amazon updated their engine, and all of a sudden their ads started to work.

Cost per clicks on my ads ran as low as 20 cents, and man did I move books. Today my average bid for top shelf keywords or for automatic ads is north of $1 a click.

Let that sink in. I'm telling Amazon that for every person who clicks on my 99-cent book, Amazon will charge me a dollar. Best case scenario I lose 67 cents because they bought the book.

What if it takes 15 clicks to get a sale? Yikes. So how can I get away with it? When I bid 1.09 or 1.13 or whatever my bid is, Amazon doesn't necessarily spend that amount. Generally my cost per click is closer to .65 or as low as .50. However, there are times when I blow through that daily ad budget in 10 clicks, and I always have to be ready for that to happen.

What makes this worse is that Amazon's reporting system is two squirrels running through pneumatic tubes carrying floppy disks. I swear. How else could it take 48-72 hours for our ads to accurately show anything? Because it can, and often does.

Amazon is a great platform, but it's very much pay to play. If you're not advertising a series you're going to struggle. There are a few niches, and some neat stuff you can do with keywords, but none of that is scalable.

I've seen people invest two hours a day for weeks, get all their ads profitable, and then when I ask them how much actual money they made, their faces fall because they realize all their work resulted in $284 of profitable sales.

No thanks. I'll stick to broad keywords, categories, and Amazon's automatic ads. My audience building happens on other platforms, where it is far more valuable.

Amazon Ad Pros

- Granular audiences
- Warm audience ready to buy books

- Easy to set up and maintain
- Automatic targeting works really well
- Great way to get visibility in Kindle Unlimited

Amazon Ad Cons

- Can burn through your budget quickly making mistakes costly
- Super saturated with authors
- Very expensive compared to other platforms

Where Do I Find Amazon Advertising?

You can log in to Amazon at https://advertising. amazon.com. This page will give you a series of options, and those options are always changing. Currently, click 'Advertising Console' and it will take you to the account connected to your KDP account.

How do I make an Ad?

Amazon is super straight forward. When you log in, you are presented with this on the upper-left-hand side of the screen:

Christopher's Account

Campaigns   Drafts   Advertising reports

Create campaign   Q Find a campaign   Filter by ⇅   ✓ 250 results

Filters: Active status = All ✕   Reset filters

Click the 'Create campaign' button, which will bring you to a screen with two options:

I almost always use 'Sponsored Products'. 'Lockscreen Ads' show up on Kindles, and on smartphones or tablets where the user has agreed to allow the Kindle app to show notifications.

These notifications are disabled for many users. I've left them on for my own phone to see what kind of books Amazon pushes, and those books have never been well targeted. Not once.

Amazon offers me thrillers, and romances, and all sorts of things outside my usual genres. It does this because the advertisers are trying to use shotgun advertising. Some small percentage of people viewing this ad might be interested, and if they reach enough of them they'll make sales. That's a very expensive way to test.

Sponsored product ads are tied much more closely to data.

Someone searches for 'Space Dragons', I bid on the 'Space Dragons' keyword, and my ad gets displayed. Or they search for 'Space Opera Books', and there I am. I can predict how and when they are shown, which makes them much more valuable to me.

Lockscreen ads can work—if you have a book with broad appeal. I've seen people make tons of money. For me though? I mostly steer clear.

When Should I Use Amazon?

Amazon ads are incredibly powerful over the long term, and it's not hard to understand why. How often do you personally use Amazon? That's replicated globally, and Amazon's strength is growing in the areas they don't currently dominate.

I run $100 - $150 a day in Amazon ads across my back catalogue. Most of that is in $5 increments, and those ads are designed to be evergreen. I haven't changed my ads for *5,000 Words Per Hour* in over 2 years. I don't need to. The ad copy is powerful, and I'm happy to pay for the same screen real estate until the end of time.

If you are a new author, though, Amazon is a quick way to drain your entire ad budget. I highly recommend limiting yourself to no more than $10 a day, and then lowering your bid per click a little each day until you are no longer spending the full $10.

Walk your ad spend back up a little bit, and park it. You've found your sweet spot.

Further Reading

If you can tolerate math, then I highly recommend *Mastering Amazon Ads* by Brian Meeks. Brian is a data geek, and his material can be a little dense, but if you want to know how to run profitable Amazon ads the right way his book does a brilliant job of breaking it down.

Exercise #10- Set Up an Amazon Ads Account

It doesn't matter if you ever plan to use it, or if you don't have a budget to spend. Basic familiarity with Amazon is important to your career as an author.

In the future, many of the organic tools we have to sell through Amazon will vanish. What you'll be left with are ads. Learn to use them well, and you will never go hungry!

Bonus: Make an audience using what you learned in the building audiences chapter. Note that your audiences are not saved separately as they are in Facebook. They are attached to a specific ad. However, you can clone that ad as often as you want, and even change the product you are advertising. In this way you can reuse Amazon audiences.

11

REDDIT ADS

Reddit ads are the reason many authors picked up this book. They haven't heard of Reddit ads, or if they have then they're eager to dive into a platform not already overrun with authors.

Let me burst that bubble right now. Reddit is a war zone. A highly opinionated war zone that hates self-promotion, even if you're paying for that promotion.

Its interface is clunky, and the platform is still changing in massive ways. Just a few weeks ago they changed it so I can no longer use cost per click on most of my ads. Now I have to pay for 1,000 impressions (CPM- cost per mil), and you can guess which side of the business arrangement is profiting from that.

However, Reddit ads do play a role in my ad spend. They're only about 10% of my overall budget, but they are a good tool for selling audiobooks, and for giving away free books. In fact, there are several subreddits (little communities) devoted specifically to free books.

If I use free days from a Kindle Countdown Deal, then I'll often run some Reddit ads in addition to making posts in the right communities.

I also find that Reddit is a great way to sell audiobooks, if you know where to peddle your wares. That knowledge represents the biggest hurdle with Reddit.

So What Is Reddit?

Reddit is a collection of user created communities called subreddits. Anyone can make a subreddit, and the person who creates it gets to be the moderator. Some of my favorite subreddits are Fantasy, Audiobooks, and Selfpublish.

Any user can submit a new post at any time. Often these are links to movie trailers, books, YouTube videos, memes, or what Reddit calls a self-post. You just put some text in, usually with the intent of starting a conversation.

One of my favorite self posts asked what you'd do if you found yourself in your body in 1990. You are you from that time, but you remember everything through today.

The answers were fascinating, and some were hilarious. Users vote up and down on these posts, and the up-voted ones quickly rise to the top.

When you log onto Reddit you see a front page that looks a lot like a Facebook feed. That feed is comprised of all the articles and content submitted to all the subreddits you belong to.

Reddit Ad Pros

- Relatively cheap cost per click or CPM
- Not yet totally overrun by authors

Reddit Ad Cons

- Clunky interface
- Audience is not as receptive to ads
- Many users have ad blockers installed
- Constant sweeping changes to how they operate

Where Do I Find It?

You can create a Reddit advertising account at https://ads.reddit.com. Note that you need an existing Reddit account.

How do I Make An Ad?

After you log into your account you'll be looking at a screen like this:

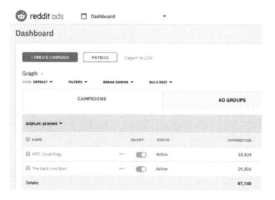

Click the 'Create Campaign' button, which will take you to a screen with a bunch of options that are similar to what we'd see in Facebook. You can experiment with these, but currently I'm getting the best CPC from conversion ads, though not by much. If I'm giving something away for free in the hopes of a mailing list sign up then I'll select 'Brand Awareness' and pay per impressions instead of clicks.

Setting up a Reddit ad isn't all that different from other platforms. The most important difference you want to be aware of is subreddits. Reddit is comprised of communities, and each community of significant size can serve as a keyword for your ads. One of the best examples is the Audiobooks subreddit. You'd plug that in under interests, in this area:

Also note that you can time gate your ads to make them run during peak hours. If you know that your readers are getting off work and looking for their next read, then you can focus your ad so it only runs during those hours.

When Should You Use Reddit?

I've made Reddit ads sound absolutely terrible, but there are some uses as mentioned above. Every time I launch an audiobook I make a Reddit ad.

Reddit users like free stuff. A fair number (though nowhere near all) are happy to pirate content. They'll sometimes link to YouTube channels with our entire back catalogues in audio.

But they do buy stuff, if they're interested. And once they become loyal to someone, they stay loyal. The Fantasy subreddit has a basket of maybe 20 authors it considers to be superstars, and every new member of that sub will receive recommendations to read them.

That sub is over a half million people. Think about that.

≈

Exercise #11- Set Up a Reddit Ads Account

Unlike the other platforms I'm not going to stress creating a Reddit account. If you don't already use Reddit then trying to learn to advertise there is a colossal waste of your time.

However, if you do use Reddit then please create an ads account.

Bonus: Make an audience using what you learned in the building audiences chapter. I'd recommend using the interests option, and only using subreddits if you can get the audience sizes over a million.

Note that your audiences are not saved separately as they are in Facebook. They are attached to a specific ad campaign. However, you can clone that campaign as often as you want. In this way you can reuse Reddit audiences.

12

BOOKBUB ADS

L et me preface this by saying that BookBub is the platform I have the least amount of experience with. That's because, in my experience, BookBub is not attracting the kind of reader I'm interested in.

As I do with all things author business, I put myself in the reader's shoes. What type of reader subscribes to BookBub?

Deal seekers. People who want free, or cheap, books. They are the absolute last type of reader I'm interested in, because they'll binge a book or two every day. They'll chew through your backlist, if they get that far, and then forget who you are, in much the same way that Kindle Unlimited readers do.

They aren't loyal to you. They're after entertainment.

Now that isn't to say every BookBub reader is like this. There are people who are more than happy to pay full price, but figure that if they're going to sample a lot of books they may as well be inexpensive ones.

More importantly, when Amazon is deciding how and when to promote your books they don't care so much where your sales come from. If a bunch of deal seeking readers pay 99 cents for your book, then you'll get the corresponding rank increase.

Once you earn a rank on Amazon, that rank is easier to keep, because it takes less sales to maintain a rank than it does to earn it. BookBub ads are great during a launch, even if they lose a little money.

I tend to dump cash into BB ads around big launches, but otherwise only run about 5% of my ad spend through them.

What Is BookBub?

BookBub is the largest free and discounted ebook newsletter in the world. You sign up, and every day BB will send you a list of books based on the genres you said you were interested in.

There's a section for free, and a section for on sale. These slots are highly coveted in the author world, because landing one means being put in front of hundreds of thousands, or even millions of readers.

In these mailers there are also paid ad spots which anyone can bid for, and that's where we come in. You want to be the little sidebar on the email. As they're scrolling past daily deals...they see your book.

Where Is It?

You can create a BookBub advertising account at http:// partners.bookbub.com/. Note that as of this writing they are still technically in beta, and there could be some delay in setting up your account. It's worth the wait, and I'd at least get the ball rolling.

This is the same account you'll use to submit your book for the much more coveted featured ad.

How Do I Make An Ad?

Once you've logged in you should see a red banner at the top that looks like this:

If you click on 'Create New Ad' you'll get a screen that looks like this:

The first thing to know about BookBub is that your ads live and die by the creative. I highly recommend making your own. You can use Book Brush, Canva, or have your neighbor's son make something in photoshop. However you get it, you want a great, original ad.

I've tried running the BookBub created ads, and they struggle because they look just like the ads most authors are using. If you want to stand out make a great creative.

Once you've got one you need to dial in your audience. BookBub has categories like Amazon as you can see:

However, the most useful targeting comes from targeting specific authors. All you have to do is type in their name, and you can see how many readers they have. Pick a dozen authors in a tightly defined niche, your niche, and start showing their readers what you have to offer.

Further Reading

I highly recommend *BookBub Ads Expert* by David Gaughran. I had the chance to sit down with Dave at NINC back in 2017, and that dude is sharp. His book gives a great high-level view of the BookBub ad platform, and note that he is one of only a few people who've managed to make those ads profitable. His book is definitely worth a look.

The short version? Discount all the previous books in a series and promote the crap out of them all. I've done it. It works. Really well.

～

Exercise #12- Set Up a BookBub Ads Account

BookBub is a platform you could skip entirely, just like Reddit. The reason I suggest you make an account anyway is that BookBub is one of the few surviving competitors to Amazon. They are a viable avenue to compete.

By running just a trickle of ads you will earn BookBub followers, and BookBub sends new release emails on your behalf to all your followers. More sales!

Bonus: Make an audience using what you learned in the Building Audiences chapter. Note that your audiences are not saved separately as they are in Facebook. They are attached to a specific campaign, more like Reddit.

PART III

ADVANCED STUFF

13

PREPARING YOUR FIRST CAMPAIGN

I t's time to bring the whole book together! If you've been doing the exercises you should now have all of the following:

- A folder full of images for your prominent keywords.
- A page full of quotes, marketing copy, or excerpts from your books.
- At least three defined audiences, which you can now split by gender, age, and region.
- A basic understanding of the four ad platforms and some idea of which one seems best for you. I'm hoping that's either Facebook or AMS, as they're great first choices.

If you don't have all these things then you won't be able to make full use of this chapter. We're going to get hands on, and we're going to make a Facebook campaign, and then an Amazon campaign.

Note that I am pushing you out of the nest. You don't get screen-by-screen walk-throughs. Instead, I'll give you the basics. You will need to locate the proper controls within the platform you wish to use.

If that sounds daunting, that's expected. It's going to take time to become familiar, but this is how you begin that process.

We Briefly Interrupt This Broadcast for Blatant Self-Promo

I know everyone hates commercials. I hate commercials. Hear me out. You're about to read the process for creating ads on Facebook and on Amazon.

There are a few hundred words of text, and several screen-shots. That's it. I don't know about you, but that isn't a lot to go on. Learning skills like this can require a more visual approach.

I do have an *Ads for Authors Who Hate Math* course. It breaks down every skill in this book in video form, so instead of a few screenshots, you get the complete hands-on walk-through.

If that sounds helpful, then you can find details at https://chris-fox-writes.teachable.com/p/ads-for-authors-who-hate-math/?product_id=1083069. If it doesn't seem worthwhile, then save yourself $100. This book covers the same skills, and you can instead invest that money in ads.

However, if you're struggling to implement what you've learned here then the course might be a good way to get it all to gel. Plus, you'll get to talk to me! I'll be doing office hours where you can get feedback on your ads, and get your questions answered.

Let's Do Facebook

I need to make an ad for the 6th book in my Magitech Chronicles series, and you're going to ride shotgun. First, we'll make a simple audience. Then, we'll make a simple ad.

For the audience I'm going to test Michael Bay's *Transformers* movies, because the visuals are very similar to my artwork. My audience ended up looking like this:

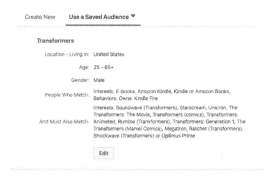

Note that I have clones of this audience based on age and gender, but you can look at the basic interests. Must match TRANSFORMERS and LIKES KINDLE. That intersection is what I'm trying to get across.

Armed with my new audience I set out to create an ad. I looked through my images, and tried to find the one I thought might work best. Facebook allows you to create six-second movies by dropping in images. It pans slowly over them like a Ken Burns documentary.

I tried experimenting with the order of those images and found this one worked the best:

When designing ads on Facebook I tend to make one campaign for each audience I'm testing, so this becomes the Transformers ad campaign.

Then, I create one ad for each image or text I want to test. If you have five or ten versions, then you can allow Facebook to adjust budgets so that the images that are converting start getting shown more.

Let's Do Amazon

Now we're going to replicate the ad for Amazon. The good news, as you'll see, is that we need way less than we do for Facebook. The only image we can use is the cover of our book, which is excellent news. It means that we're on a level playing field.

Everyone can only use covers, and if your covers are really good then you can hang with the largest authors in the world.

You start by selecting the type of campaign. I usually do Sponsored Products:

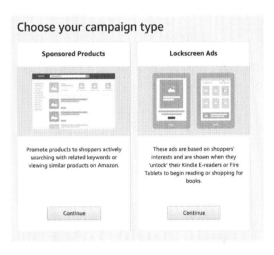

Then we choose a title, some dates, and a daily budget:

Then we select a product, usually one of our books:

Finally, we set a bid. If we selected manual targeting then we're also setting keywords here, which you are well armed with if you've done the exercises thus far:

～

Exercise #13- Make Both Ads

No bonus. No fluff. Do the work in this chapter and create one ad on Facebook and another on Amazon. Note that you do not have to actually give them any budget if you're not ready, but I recommend pulling the trigger on your ad budget as soon as you're prepared.

14

PRUNING ADS

E arlier in the book we talked about the uses of our 30-minute Time Blocks. All of those uses were detailed except for one—pruning ads. We couldn't really teach this until you had something to prune. Assuming you pulled the trigger in the last chapter—now you do!

The great news is that pruning is pretty easy, and this chapter is fairly short.

When you begin your pruning Time Block you start with the first campaign, and work your way down ad by ad. You're reviewing each one with the following checklist:

- Check the cost per click.
- Read the comments (if applicable).
- Check the Frequency (on Facebook).

That's it. You don't care about anything else.

Ad Comments

Facebook ads allow readers to leave comments. Reddit ads have them turned off by default, but you can allow users to leave them if you so choose. Depending on the type of content you're using that could be a wise move.

For example, if you're releasing a book trailer then turning comments on will allow people to gush about it, and that kind of engagement is exactly what you're after.

If, on the other hand, you've got a direct sales ad pointing at Amazon, definitely turn your comments off.

For Facebook I love having them on. I love engaging with fans. Occasionally an asshat we're going to call the mansplainer will pop up, and that's okay.

You have two choices. You can either delete the comment outright, which this user will see, or you can choose to hide it.

Always choose to hide it.

If you do this the person who left the comment will have no idea. Only that person and their friend's list will be able to see it, which is a couple hundred people out of the hundreds of thousands you're putting your ad in front of. Only delete the post if you want to antagonize that person, and be aware they can report your ads to Facebook, and Facebook tends to nuke things from orbit much like Amazon does.

Discretion is the better part of valor.

Cost Per Click

Cost per click is a near universal metric on ads, and is how I prefer to measure performance. If you're getting a low cost per click, then that platform likes your ad. They think it's a good fit for their audience, and are happy to show it repeatedly.

Below are last month's averages of my CPC on various platforms:

Amazon: .53

Facebook: .31

Reddit: .35

BookBub: .74

It should be noted that while Amazon, Facebook, and Reddit will happily spend as much money as I will give them, BookBub will not. I have to get over a dollar per click in my genres to get impressions.

They won't even show ads at .74 unless I'm carefully targeting niches off the beaten path.

Anyway, I use these numbers as a baseline. Since my Amazon average is .53, then if I have an ad getting less than that, awesome! It's doing better than average. If it's doing worse it needs to be punished. I'll typically reduce spend on anything higher than .53, unless I'm doing a rank grab during a release week.

For Facebook if they hit .32 I'll generally reduce their budget by 50%. I turn them off when they reach .40.

Frequency

Frequency is only a trackable metric on Facebook, but basically it shows you how many times your audience has seen this ad. The closer to 2.0 the more of your audience has seen it multiple times.

This doesn't distribute evenly, either. Some people have seen it seven times, and are already sick of it. Some have never seen it at all.

The higher this number the worse the ad is likely to perform. You'll notice your CPC going up as this goes up, simply because people stop reacting to an ad once they've seen it a few times.

When you are pruning look for ads that had a sudden spike in CPC. Check their frequency, or if you are on Amazon check their age. The older the ad, the less likely it will continue to perform.

If ads stop performing and have a high frequency, you can either turn them off entirely, or significantly reduce their budget.

∾

Exercise #14 - Prune Your Ads

Use a Time Block to prune your ads. This requires you to wait until you have ads, of course, which means at least a few days after your first campaign goes live.

You may be tempted to prune before then. Don't. If you set up ads, then let them run for at least 24 hours before turning them off. Especially on Amazon. Only then should you consider pruning, and if possible I'd suggest waiting 72 hours.

That does mean losing a little money, but it means being sure when you make changes to an ad. I've turned off ads prematurely and regretted it.

Bonus: Analyze the ads that you decide to prune. Why do you think their cost is higher? What's different? Is it the audience? The ad itself? If so, how could you create a new ad that might fare better?

15

TIPS & TRICKS

The goal of this book is to prepare you for a lifetime of testing and study. Hopefully after reading this far that seems less daunting, and the idea of managing your advertising through Time Blocks makes it easier to formulate a plan.

This chapter is the last practical one, and includes some of the general tools and tips I've picked up during my tenure as a self-published advertiser. Some of them are surprising, but most are fairly intuitive.

You may or may not find these trends to be true, and as always I would encourage you to decide for yourself. Never accept anything someone tells you without testing it first. Even very smart people are wrong a significant amount of the time, and even if they aren't what worked for them may not work the same way for you.

Bid High, Then Walk It Down

One of the first tricks I learned, and this is true on Amazon, Reddit, BookBub, and Facebook, is that if I first bid high, then lower my bid the ad will generate far more impressions.

The inverse is not true. If you start with a low bid, and then gradually raise it, most ad platforms won't suddenly begin showing it. You've forever hampered that ad.

When an ad is created all ad platforms are tracking a variety of metrics. When they're calculating your cost per click they're figuring out what percentage of people clicked on it, how many impressions it took before the first click, and I'm sure a bunch of things we haven't even thought of.

This system favors the ad companies, of course. If you set an ad to 67 cents a click, then you're going to burn through your ad spend quickly. You can lower it to .59 tomorrow, but you're still going to be paying through the nose for clicks until you can get those ads dialed in.

Your job is to find the sweet spot. What's the most you feel comfortable paying for a click? Stay firm, and don't go over that. If your ads aren't being shown for that bid, then you may want to consider another ad platform, or constructing a new audience.

Ads Have a Short Shelf Life

Every ad I have ever created becomes less effective over time. Much like books on Amazon are constantly being churned off the front page, ads are being churned off Facebook feeds.

Facebook wants to show fresh, relevant content. If users have seen your ad 17 times each, then they're sick of it. So Facebook raises the price on your clicks. So does Amazon. And BookBub. And Reddit. And probably the next ad platform that doesn't exist yet.

You need to constantly be changing it up. If you aren't, then your ads will languish. That's okay sometimes. Sometimes you need to disappear into your cave and crank out that next book, and your ads suffer.

I try to be diligent about my Time Blocks, but after they've slipped for a while it's important I get in there and prune, then make new ads. Ads have a short shelf life. Watch them carefully, and kill them when they start getting too expensive per click.

You get to decide what that threshold is, but if your ads go over it, then kill them, and make new ones.

Pixels & Retargeting

We mentioned Facebook targeting pixels earlier in the book, and gave you some idea of how they work. A pixel is an identifier that matches a specific user, and tracks their activity across the web. It follows them, as a literal spy.

Then that spy cheerfully reports its findings when the user arrives at Facebook. Facebook responds by showing that person whatever it thinks they'll buy, based on the web sites they were just browsing.

This is INCREDIBLY POWERFUL. Creepy, but powerful. Let's take my Magitech Chronicles, and I'll show you how.

I start by creating a link to some worldbuilding for the setting, like this one:

Each one of these ads gives them something, and asks nothing. Here's a new character from the series with complete stats. Here's the new spells we've created. Here's some new artwork we just received.

People who like the setting click those links. All the time. Why wouldn't they? I do whenever something I'm interested in pops up.

Meanwhile Facebook is quietly building a list of everyone who's engaged with your ads. When I launch the 7th book in the series I can build an audience that includes everyone who ever engaged with my other ads.

This makes telling people about sequels much, much easier, and can reinforce your mailers to dramatically increase early conversion. That will get you more rank, which will drive more early sales, and accelerate Amazon's learning.

Pixels can be intimidating, and they're only available on

Facebook for now. If that isn't your chosen platform then you won't need to worry about this tactic.

Exercise #15- The Last One

Select your next tool. Maybe that's a book on a specific ad platform, like Michael Cooper's *Help! My Facebook Ads Suck*, or Dave's *BookBub Ads Expert*.

Maybe it's a course, like the one I'm shamelessly promoting. Maybe it's joining a community of authors who are in the same boat you are, trying to figure it all out.

The important take away is to **take action**. Continue your learning. Keep trying to master ads. This is a skill that requires constant improvement, and like writing it can feel like it's taking you forever to "get it."

Put in the time. Put in the study. Let's get rich telling stories. =D

Bonus: Set a reminder for one week, and another for one month. The text of that reminder should ask, "How are your ads doing?"

16

THE LAST CHAPTER

This chapter remains my favorite to write, because it's my chance to have an open dialogue with authors. I've done this seven times now with the other books in this series, and if you look at just the last chapters you can see my own evolution as an author.

When I started in 2014 it was enough to write fast, provided you were publishing professional books. If you got out 4+ books a year, and the covers weren't terrible, then you could make a profit.

If you knew about writing to market back then you could clear mid six figures, and so many people were. A BookBub could keep your backlist afloat for weeks. Months, in some cases.

By 2016 the game was starting to change. Lots of frustrated authors had a half-dozen books out, but weren't selling. One by one they dropped out, or figured out how to iterate. They improved their covers, or discovered writing to market.

By 2018 the market was starting to tighten. Now if you want

to break the top 20 of most genres you need ad spend, and you need contacts with other big authors in your genre.

Breaking out has become more rare, though I still see it happen all the time. Often with little or no ad spend. But that's a lightning strike now, whereas it used to be business as usual.

By 2020 the market will be tighter still. Every book published from 2011, when the gold rush began, to the present is still there. Every big hit. Every long running series.

Every author is now battling to get their backlist seen, and to get their new releases to the front page. That battle will intensify, and eventually, by say 2022, or 2025, your average author will no longer be able to compete.

Doing so will require tens of thousands of dollars of ad spend annually, and margins will get thinner and thinner. It will become more and more difficult to make a splash.

So what does this mean for you? You are in exactly the right place, at the right time. The market is still settling, still learning. Tools are still being developed. Companies are still forming.

You're at the ground level. If you can master ads, and do it in 2019, then when the market is brutally oppressive in 2025 not only will you know who your audience is, and how to reach them, but you'll have a large backlist with which to do so.

You'll be a survivor.

The other option is to accept that being an author long term will be more about running your business than writing your books. One of my next books tackles running your author business, and doing it efficiently.

Even with every tip and trick in my arsenal, though, I've come to realize that advertising and marketing is a full time job. I need an assistant. I can't do everything forever if I want to keep growing.

But you know what? I don't have to. I can hire an assistant, give them this book, and the *Ads for Authors Who Hate Math* course, and then turn them loose. I can teach them to do what I do, and then we can add a new type of Time Block.

We'll call that block Management, and that will involve my advertiser giving me a report on my ads. If it works...expect a book or video showing the process!

Hopefully you see what I'm doing here. I'm committed to growth. I'm committed to learning new skills, and to making my business more efficient. That's a survival skill.

As our market matures those with inefficient business models will either fail, or fall back to doing this part time. Those with efficient business models will retire telling stories that they love.

I'm going to be in the second group, and I hope that you will too. I hope that you're fired up. I hope that you're ready to start conquering advertising.

It won't be easy, and it won't be cheap. Learning to advertise and advertise well is an enormous challenge. It's one not every author will succeed at. But you now have the tools and the system.

Get out there and kill it.

If you find that this book isn't enough, and want to take it to the next level, then give the course a look. I'd love to meet you, and to help you get to where you want to be as an author.

-Chris

LEXICON

This chapter contains a short list of the commonly used acronyms in this book. If you see anything that should be added please let me know by sending an email to chris@chrisfoxwrites.com. We'll get it added!

Cost Per Click- Cost per click. This measures how much you're paying for each click, and goes up the more impressions it takes to generate a click.

Read-through- The percentage of readers who continue past the first book into sequels. This number will be different for each sequel in a series.

Landing Page- A website you create that is designed to get readers to sign up to your mailing list. This page should have no links except for the one that allows them to sign up.

CPM- Cost Per Mil (1,000). Some ad platforms allow you to spend based on impressions, not clicks. You pay for them regardless of whether you get any clicks, which isn't as bad as it sounds.

Negative Keyword- Sometimes you want to exclude a search term in your ads. This can be done both on Facebook and Amazon, and allows you to eliminate words you don't want. I commonly use "Harem" and "Romance" as negative keywords, because my books have neither of those things.

Ad Campaign- A bucket to hold ads. Usually this campaign has a theme, like a specific audience, or a specific book it is advertising. How this is structured is up to the person doing the advertising.

CTR- Click-through rate. This is the percentage of people who click an ad. If 1,000 people see it, and 10 click it, then you have a 1% CTR. A 4% CTR is amazing, in my experience.

EXERCISES

Exercise #1- Commit to a Monthly Budget

Take a hard look at your cover and your blurb. Are they good enough? Show them to other successful authors in your genre, and see what they say.

If, and only if, they agree that your cover rocks, then decide on an affordable dollar amount. How much can you spend every month? $50? $500? Zero? The answer will be different for every author, and that's okay.

Come up with yours. Remember that this money will be lost every month. It's gone. Maybe you'll make some sales and maybe you won't. Treat this like an expense, and set it at a level you're comfortable with.

Bonus: Break your ad spend down by series. How much does each part of your backlist get? Why?

∼

Exercise #2- Calculate Your Gross Profit

Add up all revenue you earned from your books. This should include audio, print, and ebook.

Now add up all money you spent on marketing and advertising. Include every penny. Boosted Facebook posts, BookBub, AMS, whatever you spent rolls into that total.

Compare the numbers. Have you made a profit as an author?

Bonus: Break down each series and genre you write. How much did you spend to advertise each, and how much did you make? Which books or series are carrying your backlist?

~

Exercise #3- Schedule Your Time Blocks

Where can you carve out 30 minutes each day? If that's too daunting right now, then pick three days a week and schedule 30 minutes. That's 90 minutes a week you're investing in your future as an author.

Bonus: Add a tag to each Time Block telling you which activity you're going to work on. Are you building audiences? Pruning ads? Creating your first campaign? Lay it out in advance.

~

Exercise #4- Build Your First Audience

Review this chapter carefully, then create your first audience. Note that you don't have to plug this into any advertising platform, and can just jot it down on a napkin if you like.

The goal is to define an audience, then replicate it by age and gender. However, if you think you're going to use Facebook, or Amazon, or Bookbub, then try building the audience there.

You'll begin learning the system for the relevant platform. Age isn't used anywhere but Facebook or Google Adwords, but it's still worth having some idea as to the age of your ideal reader for those platforms.

Bonus: Define three audiences instead of just one. You're going to need them.

Exercise #5- Gather Some Images

Make a list of words that represent your genre. These can be freeform, and more is better. Put on some music and go nuts. Here's 60 seconds from one of my series:

Dragons
Spaceships
Marines
Gods
Magic
Stars

Astronomy
Spells
Fighters
EVA
Aliens

Your list can be much longer, but make sure you have at least ten. What are the cornerstones of your genre? Rank your keywords in what you're guessing will be the order of popularity.

Find at least three pieces of artwork for the top three on your list, even if you can't afford to purchase them at this time.

Bonus: Replicate this for the entire list. The more artwork you have to test, the better.

∾

Exercise #6- Write Some Taglines

What kind of tagline will your audience respond to? Can you use longing or loathing? Which will work better? Write 10 taglines using either longing or loathing, whichever you think will work better.

Bonus: Write 10 taglines for either longing or loathing, whichever you didn't already do. The goal is to practice both. By making a bunch of each you'll force yourself to consider your plot or content from many different angles, which has a high likelihood of jarring loose a great phrase you can use.

Exercise #7- Create Your First Campaign

Decide whether you are aiming at sales or sign-ups. You can actually create the campaign on a live platform if you've already got a one picked out. Note that you don't have to turn this campaign on, or give it any budget yet.

If you don't have a platform picked out that's okay. Create a document in whatever format you'd like to use (I love Google Sheets). Pick one type of ad from the list below:

- Sales Copy
- Quote
- Excerpt
- Comparison

Write three variants of that ad. That can mean finding three quotes, three excerpts, three comparisons, or three different sales copies, but make sure all three are of the same type.

Bonus: I highly recommend doing this step. Create three ads for each of the other types, even if you don't think you will ever use that type. Learning how to generate that copy is building a vital skill. Practice this often, and always be increasing the size of your marketing document.

Exercise #8- Calculate Read-Through

If you only have one book out, or aren't enrolled in Kindle Unlimited, congrats! You get a pass.

If you have more than one book, and those books are in a series, then use the formula above to determine how much money you'll make for a sale, and how much you'll make for a read-through.

Also figure out what percentage of your revenue comes from sales versus page reads.

There is no bonus.

$\sim$

Exercise #9- Set Up a Facebook Ads Account

It doesn't matter if you ever plan to use it, or if you don't have a budget to spend on Facebook. Basic familiarity with this ad platform could be important to your career as an author. Lots of people use it, and it isn't likely to change soon.

Note that this requires you to have a Facebook account.

Bonus: Make and save three audiences in Facebook using what you learned in the building audiences chapter. If it's unclear how to do this go to Google and search for "Make Facebook Audience 20XX" where XX is the year.

Yes, I could include the information here, but you need to be able to research topics, and this is great practice.

Exercise #10- Set Up an Amazon Ads Account

It doesn't matter if you ever plan to use it, or if you don't have a budget to spend. Basic familiarity with Amazon is important to your career as an author.

In the future, many of the organic tools we have to sell through Amazon will vanish. What you'll be left with are ads. Learn to use them well, and you will never go hungry!

Bonus: Make an audience using what you learned in the building audiences chapter. Note that your audiences are not saved separately as they are in Facebook. They are attached to a specific ad. However, you can clone that ad as often as you want, and even change the product you are advertising. In this way you can reuse Amazon audiences.

Exercise #11- Set Up a Reddit Ads Account

Unlike the other platforms I'm not going to stress creating a Reddit account. If you don't already use Reddit then trying to learn to advertise there is a colossal waste of your time.

However, if you do use Reddit then please create an ads account.

Bonus: Make an audience using what you learned in the building audiences chapter. I'd recommend using the interests option, and only using subreddits if you can get the audience sizes over a million.

Note that your audiences are not saved separately as they are in Facebook. They are attached to a specific ad campaign. However, you can clone that campaign as often as you want. In this way you can reuse Reddit audiences.

~

Exercise #12- Set Up a BookBub Ads Account

BookBub is a platform you could skip entirely, just like Reddit. The reason I suggest you make an account anyway is that BookBub is one of the few surviving competitors to Amazon. They are a viable avenue to compete.

By running just a trickle of ads you will earn BookBub followers, and BookBub sends new release emails on your behalf to all your followers. More sales!

Bonus: Make an audience using what you learned in the Building Audiences chapter. Note that your audiences are not saved separately as they are in Facebook. They are attached to a specific campaign, more like Reddit.

~

Exercise #13- Make Both Ads

No bonus. No fluff. Do the work in this chapter and create one ad on Facebook and another on Amazon. Note that you do not have to actually give them any budget if you're not ready, but I recommend pulling the trigger on your ad budget as soon as you're prepared.

Exercise #14 - Prune Your Ads

Use a Time Block to prune your ads. This requires you to wait until you have ads, of course, which means at least a few days after your first campaign goes live.

You may be tempted to prune before then. Don't. If you set up ads, then let them run for at least 24 hours before turning them off. Especially on Amazon. Only then should you consider pruning, and if possible I'd suggest waiting 72 hours.

That does mean losing a little money, but it means being sure when you make changes to an ad. I've turned off ads prematurely and regretted it.

Bonus: Analyze the ads that you decide to prune. Why do you think their cost is higher? What's different? Is it the audience? The ad itself? If so, how could you create a new ad that might fare better?

Exercise #15- The Last One

Select your next tool. Maybe that's a book on a specific ad platform, like Michael Cooper's *Help! My Facebook Ads Suck*, or Dave's *BookBub Ads Expert*.

Maybe it's a course, like the one I'm shamelessly promoting. Maybe it's joining a community of authors who are in the same boat you are, trying to figure it all out.

The important take away is to **take action**. Continue your learning. Keep trying to master ads. This is a skill that requires constant improvement, and like writing it can feel like it's taking you forever to "get it."

Put in the time. Put in the study. Let's get rich telling stories. =D

Bonus: Set a reminder for one week, and another for one month. The text of that reminder should ask, "How are your ads doing?"

41386907R00072

Printed in Poland
by Amazon Fulfillment
Poland Sp. z o.o., Wrocław